Improve your scales!

A workbook for examinations

Violin Grade 3

Paul Harris

Contents

© 1996 by Faber Music Ltd
First published in 1996 by Faber Music Ltd
Revised impression 2000
3 Queen Square London WC1N 3AU
Music and text typeset by Silverfen
Cover illustration by Drew Hillier
Printed in England by Caligraving Ltd
All rights reserved

ISBN 0-571-51664-5

To buy Faber Music publications or to find out about the full range of titles
available please contact your local retailer or Faber Music sales enquiries:

Faber Music Limited, Burnt Mill, Elizabeth Way, Harlow, CM20 2HX England
Tel: +44 (0)1279 82 89 82   Fax: +44 (0)1279 82 89 83
sales@fabermusic.com   www.fabermusic.com

FABER *ff* MUSIC

Introduction

To the student

Have you ever realised that it is much easier to learn something if you *want* to? Do you ever forget your telephone number? How many characters can you name from your favourite 'soap' or football team? Scales are not difficult to learn if you really want to learn them. Not only will they improve many aspects of your technique, but you will also get high marks in the scale section of grade exams, you will be able to learn pieces more quickly (difficult passages are often nothing more than scale patterns) and your sight-reading will improve too! Treat scales as friends – they will pay you great dividends!

To the teacher

Scales and arpeggios are often a real stumbling block for exam candidates and budding musicians. **Improve your scales!** is designed to make scale preparation and learning fun!

Working through the book will encourage your pupils to approach scales and arpeggios methodically and thoughtfully. It will help with memory problems and turn scale-learning into an enjoyable experience.

Simultaneous learning
Scales, sight-reading and aural are often the aspects of teaching relegated to the final few minutes of a lesson. The link between scales (particularly in the development of 'key-sense' and the recognition of melodic/harmonic patterns) and sight-reading is obvious, and there are many ways to integrate aural into the process too. Thus the use of the material in this book as a more central feature of a lesson is strongly recommended, especially when used in conjunction with **Improve Your Sight-reading!** Pupils will learn to become more musically aware, make fewer mistakes and allow the teacher to concentrate on teaching the music!

Using this book

The purpose of this workbook is to incorporate regular scale playing into lessons and daily practice and to help pupils prepare for grade examinations. You need not work at all sections, nor in the order as set out, but the best results may well be achieved by adhering fairly closely to the material.

Know the Notes! is to prove that the actual notes *are* known! Students should be encouraged to say the notes up and down until this can be done *really* fluently. Understanding the pattern of tones and semitones is essential for the progressing violinist – in particular knowing where the semitones are within a scale and being able to hear them accurately. The shaded boxes represent the semitones and will be a useful aid in the development of this ability.

The **Finger Fitness** exercises are to give practice in putting the fingers down precisely and accurately. Consider the finger pattern before each exercise is played and always encourage an active awareness of intonation. It is recommended that these exercises are played slowly until real control is achieved. When they are fluent you may like to add dynamic levels and vary the rhythmic patterns.

The **Scale Study** and **Arpeggio Study** are really extended exercises, but place the material in a more musical and 'fun' context. Some have *ad lib.* accompaniments or you might like to improvise a simple piano accompaniment; this would add interest and help the student with intonation and timing.

Have a go is to encourage thought 'in the key', through the improvisation or composition of a short tune.

Choose a tune is to develop further the ability to think in a key. Encourage pupils to play (by ear) a well-known melody: for example Happy Birthday or the National Anthem (major), 'Greensleeves' or 'God rest ye merry gentlemen' (minor). You might like to ask pupils to improvise a simple variation on their chosen melody. This could be rhythmic or dynamic to begin. As they grow in confidence they might try 'decorating' the melody.

Say → Think → Play! is where the student finally plays the scale and arpeggio. The following method should really help in memorising each scale and arpeggio:

1 **Say** the notes out loud, up and down, and repeat until fluent.

2 **Think** through the finger patterns (but don't play out loud).

3 Think the notes and **play** the scale/arpeggio. By this time there should be no doubt in the player's mind and there should certainly be no fumbles or wrong notes!

Marking

A marking system has been included to help you and the student to monitor progress and to act as a means of encouragement. It is suggested you adopt a grading system as follows:

A Excellent work!

B Good work, but keep at it!

C A little more practice would be a good idea!

D No time to lose – get practising at once!

Revision

At the end of each stage you will find a **Revision Practice** table. As the new scales become more familiar you will wish your student to revise them regularly. This table is to encourage a methodical approach to scale practice, and show that there are endless ways of practising scales and arpeggios! Fill out the table for each week, or each practice session as follows:

1 Mark **S** for slurred or **B** for separate bows.

2 Choose a different rhythmic pattern each time from the following:

Scales:

Arpeggios:

3 Choose a different dynamic level. As students get into the habit of good scale and arpeggio practice they should no longer need the table.

Fingering

The suggested fingerings given at the back of the book are appropriate for the preparation of scales and arpeggios for examination purposes, but need not be followed strictly. Fingerings are deliberately not given elsewhere to allow teachers and pupils to adopt their own.

Group teaching

Improve your scales! is ideal for group teaching. Members of the group should be asked to comment on performances of the **Finger Fitness** exercises – was the tone even? Was the pulse even? *etc.* Exercises could be split between two or more players (e.g. playing alternate phrases), and constructive criticism should be encouraged for the scale and arpeggio studies. With the optional *ad lib.* parts, a small group of the pieces could be performed at a private 'group concert', or even at a more formal concert.

The author wishes to thank Gillian Secret and Jane Page for many helpful suggestions.

G major   2 octaves

Know the Notes!

1 Write the key signature of G major:

2 Write out the notes of the scale:

3 The semitones are between: and

4 Write out the notes of the arpeggio:

Finger Fitness

The **Finger Fitness** exercises are to give you practice in putting your fingers down precisely and accurately. Consider the finger pattern before each exercise is played. Listen carefully to intonation. These exercises should be played slowly until real control is achieved.

Galloping

Scale study in G major

Giraffe

Arpeggio study in G major

| Player 2 (ad lib.) | | Player 3 (ad lib.) |

Have a go

Compose or improvise your own tune in G major. If you are writing your tune down, remember to put in some markings and then give your piece a title.

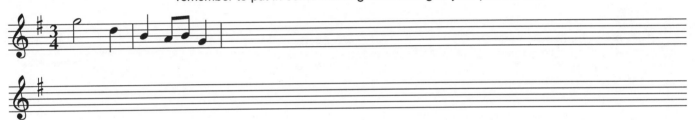

Choose a tune

Choose a well-known tune and play it in the key of G major. Now try improvising a simple variation on your chosen tune (see Introduction).

Say
Think
Play!

Say the notes out loud, up and down

Think through the finger patterns

Play the scale/arpeggio

Revision Practice

G major (2 octaves)		1	2	3	4	5	6	7	8	9	10
Scale	Slurred or separate bows										
	Rhythmic pattern										
	Dynamic										
Arpeggio	Rhythmic pattern										
	Dynamic										

Marking

G major (2 octaves)	Grade
Know the notes!	
Finger fitness	
Scale study	
Arpeggio study	
Have a go	
Choose a tune	
Say → think → play!	

6

A major   *2 octaves*

Know the Notes!

1 Write the key signature of A major:

2 Write out the notes of the scale:

3 The semitones are between: ☐☐ and ☐☐

4 Write out the notes of the arpeggio:

Finger Fitness

Autumn

Scale study in A major

Athletic Arpeggios

Arpeggio study in A major

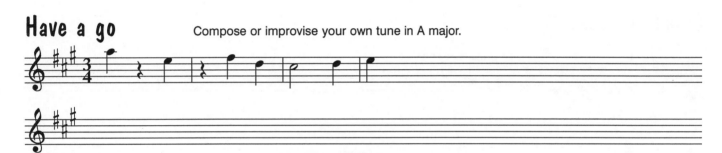

Player 2
(ad lib.)

Have a go

Compose or improvise your own tune in A major.

Choose a tune

Choose a well-known tune and play it in the key of A major. Now try improvising a simple variation on your chosen tune.

Say Think Play!

Say the notes out loud, up and down

Think through the finger patterns

Play the scale/arpeggio

Revision Practice

A major (2 octaves)		1	2	3	4	5	6	7	8	9	10
Scale	Slurred or separate bows										
	Rhythmic pattern										
	Dynamic										
Arpeggio	Rhythmic pattern										
	Dynamic										

Marking

A major (2 octaves)	Grade
Know the notes!	
Finger fitness	
Scale study	
Arpeggio study	
Have a go	
Choose a tune	
Say → think → play!	

E major   1 octave

Know the Notes!

1 Write the key signature of E major:

2 Write out the notes of the scale:

3 The semitones are between: and

4 Write out the notes of the arpeggio:

Finger Fitness

Easter Egg   Scale study in E major

Energetic Eskimos

Arpeggio study in E major

Have a go

Compose or improvise your own tune in E major.

Choose a tune

Choose a well-known tune and play it in the key of E major. Now try improvising a simple variation on your chosen tune.

Say
Think
Play!

Say the notes out loud, up and down

Think through the finger patterns

Play the scale/arpeggio

Revision Practice

E major (1 octave)		1	2	3	4	5	6	7	8	9	10
Scale	Slurred or separate bows										
	Rhythmic pattern										
	Dynamic										
Arpeggio	Rhythmic pattern										
	Dynamic										

Marking

E major (1 octave)	Grade
Know the notes!	
Finger fitness	
Scale study	
Arpeggio study	
Have a go	
Choose a tune	
Say → think → play!	

B♭ major   2 octaves

Know the Notes!

1 Write the key signature of B♭ major:

2 Write out the notes of the scale:

3 The semitones are between: and

4 Write out the notes of the arpeggio:

Finger Fitness

Boating

Scale study in B♭ major

Moderato

f   *p*   *cresc.*

6

f

11

rall.

Brontosaurus   Arpeggio study in Bb major

Have a go   Compose or improvise your own tune in Bb major.

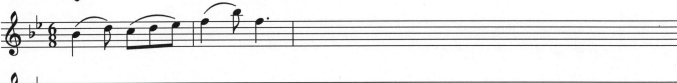

Choose a tune   Choose a well-known tune and play it in the key of Bb major. Now try improvising a simple variation on your chosen tune.

Say Think Play!

Say the notes out loud, up and down

Think through the finger patterns

Play the scale/arpeggio

Revision Practice

Bb major (2 octaves)		1	2	3	4	5	6	7	8	9	10
Scale	Slurred or separate bows										
	Rhythmic pattern										
	Dynamic										
Arpeggio	Rhythmic pattern										
	Dynamic										

Marking

Bb major (2 octaves)	Grade
Know the notes!	
Finger fitness	
Scale study	
Arpeggio study	
Have a go	
Choose a tune	
Say → think → play!	

D major   2 octaves

Know the Notes!

1 Write the key signature of D major:

2 Write out the notes of the scale:

3 The semitones are between: and

4 Write out the notes of the arpeggio:

Finger Fitness

Dastardly Dance   Scale study in D major

Allegro con fuoco

Dozy Dog

Arpeggio study in D major

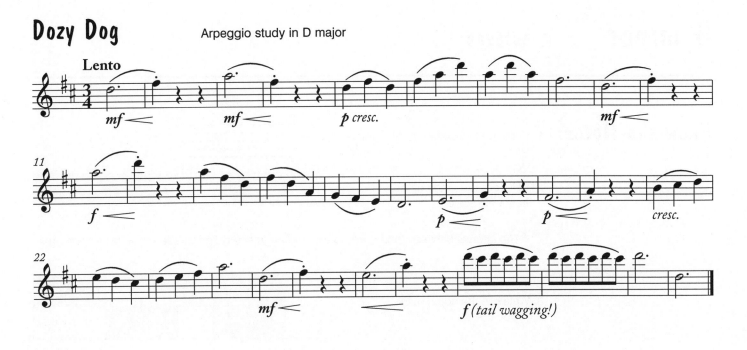

Have a go

Compose or improvise your own tune in D major.

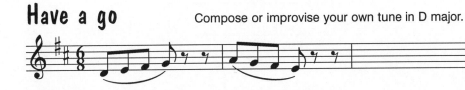

Choose a tune

Choose a well-known tune and play it in the key of D major. Now try improvising a simple variation on your chosen tune.

Say
Think
Play!

Say the notes out loud, up and down

Think through the finger patterns

Play the scale/arpeggio

Revision Practice

D major (2 octaves)		1	2	3	4	5	6	7	8	9	10
Scale	Slurred or separate bows										
	Rhythmic pattern										
	Dynamic										
Arpeggio	Rhythmic pattern										
	Dynamic										

Marking

D major (2 octaves)	Grade
Know the notes!	
Finger fitness	
Scale study	
Arpeggio study	
Have a go	
Choose a tune	
Say → think → play!	

G minor   2 octaves

Know the Notes!

1 Write the key signature of G minor:

2 Write out the notes of the harmonic scale:

* The interval between these two notes is an *augmented 2nd*, made up of three semitones.

3 Write out the notes of the melodic scale:

4 Write out the notes of the arpeggio:

Finger Fitness

Revise the exercises for G minor, 1 octave (**Improve your scales!** Violin Grades 1-2)

Graceful Ghost
Scale study in G harmonic minor

Grumpy
Scale study in G melodic minor

Gruesome Gravy
Arpeggio study in G minor

Have a go

Compose or improvise your own tune using the notes of G harmonic minor.

Have another go

Compose or improvise your own tune using the notes of G melodic minor.

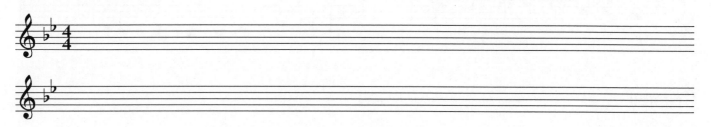

Choose a tune

Choose a well-known tune and play it in the key of G minor. Now try improvising a simple variation on your chosen tune.

Say Think Play!

Say the notes out loud, up and down

Think through the finger patterns

Play the scale/arpeggio

Revision Practice

G minor (2 octaves)		1	2	3	4	5	6	7	8	9	10
Scale	Slurred or separate bows										
	Rhythmic pattern										
	Dynamic										
Arpeggio	Rhythmic pattern										
	Dynamic										

Marking

G minor (2 octaves)	Grade
Know the notes!	
Finger fitness	
Scale study (harmonic)	
Scale study (melodic)	
Arpeggio study	
Have a go/Have another go	
Choose a tune	
Say → think → play!	

A minor 2 octaves

Know the Notes!

1 Write the key signature of A minor:

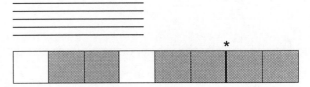

2 Write out the notes of the harmonic scale:

*The interval between these two notes is an *augmented 2nd*, made up of three semitones.

3 Write out the notes of the melodic scale:

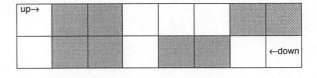

up→ ... ←down

4 Write out the notes of the arpeggio:

Finger Fitness

Revise the exercises for A minor, 1 octave (**Improve your scales!** Violin Grades 1-2)

April

Scale study in A harmonic minor

Agitated Aardvark

Scale study in A melodic minor

Afternoon Amble

Arpeggio study in A minor

Have a go

Compose or improvise your own tune using the notes of A harmonic minor.

Have another go

Compose or improvise your own tune using the notes of A melodic minor.

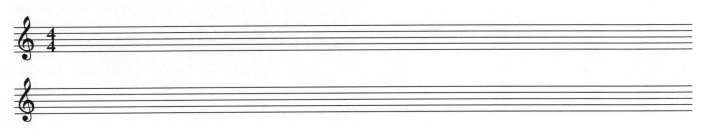

Choose a tune

Choose a well-known tune and play it in the key of A minor. Now try improvising a simple variation on your chosen tune.

Say Think Play!

Say the notes out loud, up and down

Think through the finger patterns

Play the scale/arpeggio

Revision Practice

A minor (2 octaves)		1	2	3	4	5	6	7	8	9	10
Scale	Slurred or separate bows										
	Rhythmic pattern										
	Dynamic										
Arpeggio	Rhythmic pattern										
	Dynamic										

Marking

A minor (2 octaves)	Grade
Know the notes!	
Finger fitness	
Scale study (harmonic)	
Scale study (melodic)	
Arpeggio study	
Have a go/Have another go	
Choose a tune	
Say → think → play!	

E minor   1 octave

Know the Notes!

1 Write the key signature of E minor:

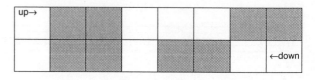

2 Write out the notes of the harmonic scale:

* The interval between these two notes is an *augmented 2nd*, made up of three semitones.

3 Write out the notes of the melodic scale:

up→

←down

4 Write out the notes of the arpeggio:

Finger Fitness

Evening

Scale study in E harmonic minor

Esther's Elegy

Scale study in E melodic minor

Epic

Arpeggio study in E minor

Have a go

Compose or improvise your own tune using the notes of E harmonic minor.

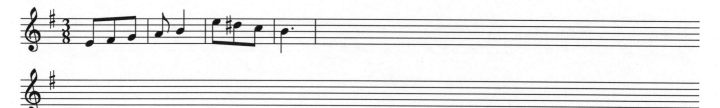

Have another go

Compose or improvise your own tune using the notes of E melodic minor.

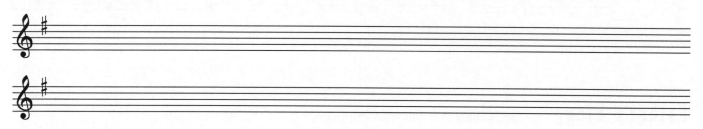

Choose a tune

Choose a well-known tune and play it in the key of E minor. Now try improvising a simple variation on your chosen tune.

Say Think Play!

Say the notes out loud, up and down

Think through the finger patterns

Play the scale/arpeggio

Revision Practice

E minor (1 octave)		1	2	3	4	5	6	7	8	9	10
Scale	Slurred or separate bows										
	Rhythmic pattern										
	Dynamic										
Arpeggio	Rhythmic pattern										
	Dynamic										

Marking

E minor (1 octave)	Grade
Know the notes!	
Finger fitness	
Scale study (harmonic)	
Scale study (melodic)	
Arpeggio study	
Have a go/Have another go	
Choose a tune	
Say → think → play!	

B♭ minor   2 octaves

Know the Notes!

1 Write the key signature of B♭ minor:

2 Write out the notes of the harmonic scale:

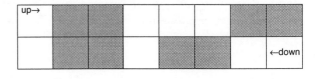

*The interval between these two notes is an *augmented 2nd*, made up of three semitones.

3 Write out the notes of the melodic scale:

4 Write out the notes of the arpeggio:

Finger Fitness

Ballad

Scale study in Bb harmonic minor

Brandy Butter

Scale study in Bb melodic minor

Burlesque

Arpeggio study in Bb minor

Have a go

Compose or improvise your own tune using the notes of Bb harmonic minor.

Have another go

Compose or improvise your own tune using the notes of Bb melodic minor.

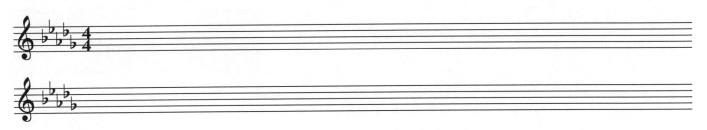

Choose a tune

Choose a well-known tune and play it in the key of Bb minor. Now try improvising a simple variation on your chosen tune.

Say Think Play!

Say the notes out loud, up and down

Think through the finger patterns

Play the scale/arpeggio

Revision Practice

Bb minor (2 octaves)		1	2	3	4	5	6	7	8	9	10
Scale	Slurred or separate bows										
	Rhythmic pattern										
	Dynamic										
Arpeggio	Rhythmic pattern										
	Dynamic										

Marking

Bb minor (2 octaves)	Grade
Know the notes!	
Finger fitness	
Scale study (harmonic)	
Scale study (melodic)	
Arpeggio study	
Have a go/Have another go	
Choose a tune	
Say → think → play!	

D minor   *2 octaves*

Know the Notes!

1 Write the key signature of D minor:

2 Write out the notes of the
   harmonic scale:

*The interval between these two notes is an *augmented 2nd*, made up of three semitones.

3 Write out the notes of the
   melodic scale:

4 Write out the notes of the arpeggio:

Finger Fitness

Revise the exercises for D minor, 1 octave (**Improve your scales!** Violin Grades 1-2)

Doleful Dolphin   Scale study in D harmonic minor

Dragonfly   Scale study in D melodic minor

Dance   Arpeggio study in D minor

Have a go

Compose or improvise your own tune using the notes of D harmonic minor.

Have another go

Compose or improvise your own tune using the notes of D melodic minor.

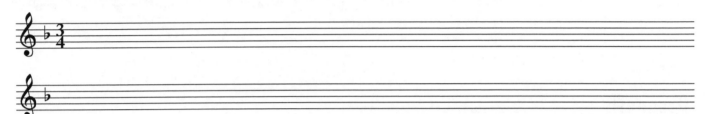

Choose a tune

Choose a well-known tune and play it in the key of D minor. Now try improvising a simple variation on your chosen tune.

Say Think Play!

Say the notes out loud, up and down

Think through the finger patterns

Play the scale/arpeggio

Revision Practice

D minor (2 octaves)		1	2	3	4	5	6	7	8	9	10
Scale	Slurred or separate bows										
	Rhythmic pattern										
	Dynamic										
Arpeggio	Rhythmic pattern										
	Dynamic										

Marking

D minor (2 octaves)	Grade
Know the notes!	
Finger fitness	
Scale study (harmonic)	
Scale study (melodic)	
Arpeggio study	
Have a go/Have another go	
Choose a tune	
Say → think → play!	

Scales

> **SCALES (exam requirements of the Associated Board)**
> From memory, in the following keys:
>
> E major; E minor (one octave)
> G, A, Bb, D majors; G, A, Bb, D minors (two octaves)
>
> **Scales:** in the above keys (minors in melodic *or* harmonic form at candidate's choice):
> (i) separate bows
> (ii) slurred, with two quavers to a bow
>
> **Chromatic Scales:** starting on open strings G, D and A (one octave): separate bows, even notes

G major   (2 octaves)

*separate bows

*slurred

A major   (2 octaves)

E major   (1 octave)

*Slurred and separate bows required for all major and minor scales.

B♭ major   (2 octaves)

D major   (2 octaves)

3rd pos. restez

G minor   (2 octaves)

harmonic

melodic

A minor   (2 octaves)

harmonic

melodic

E minor   (1 octave)

harmonic

melodic

B♭ minor   (2 octaves)

D minor   (2 octaves)

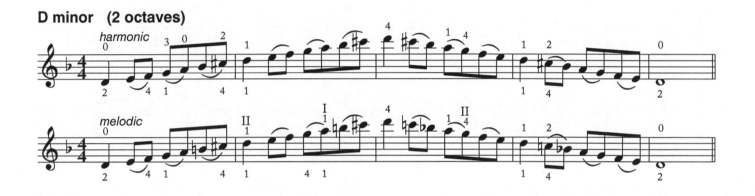

Chromatic scales

Starting on G

Starting on D

Starting on A

Arpeggios

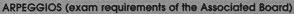

ARPEGGIOS (exam requirements of the Associated Board)
From memory, in the following keys:

    E major; E minor (one octave)
    G, A, B♭, D majors; G, A, B♭, D minors (two octaves)

Arpeggios: the common chords of the above keys:
(i) separate bows, even notes
(ii) slurred, three notes to a bow

Dominant Sevenths: in the keys of C, G and D (starting on open strings G, D and A and resolving on the tonic) (one octave): separate bows, even notes

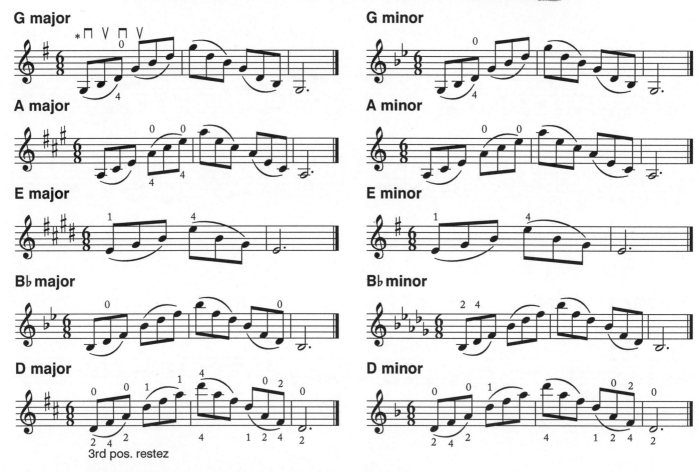

G major

G minor

A major

A minor

E major

E minor

B♭ major

B♭ minor

D major

3rd pos. restez

D minor

*Slurred and separate bows required for all major and minor arpeggios.

Dominant sevenths

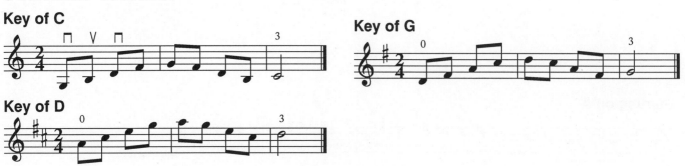

Key of C

Key of G

Key of D